H
Handle Your
Exam
Nerves

HOW TO HANDLE YOUR EXAM NERVES

Katherine Bebo has asserted her moral right to be identified as the author of this work in accordance with sections 77 and 78 of the Copyright, Designs and Patents Act 1988.

An Hachette UK Company
www.hachette.co.uk

Vie Books, an imprint of Summersdale Publishers Ltd
Part of Octopus Publishing Group Limited
Carmelite House
50 Victoria Embankment
LONDON
EC4Y 0DZ
UK

www.summersdale.com

Printed and bound in Malta

ISBN: 978-1-78783-649-5

DISCLAIMER
The author and the publisher cannot accept responsibility for any misuse or misunderstanding of any information contained herein, or any loss, damage or injury, be it health, financial or otherwise, suffered by any individual or group acting upon or relying on information contained herein. None of the views or suggestions in this book is intended to replace professional opinion from someone who is familiar with your particular circumstances. If you have concerns about your health or well-being, please seek professional advice.

How to Handle Your Exam Nerves

Study Tips and Healthy Habits for Confidence and Success

Katherine Bebo

Contents

Introduction

So, your exams are getting close. How are you feeling? Worried? Confident? Fed up? Fired up? All of the above? Preparing for exams is a testing time. "*Will I pass? What if I don't get high enough grades? What if I die of boredom while working on simultaneous equations?*" These are all valid concerns, but freaking out won't get you anywhere. To bring your A-game to your exams, what you need is a plan – and that's where this book comes in. From constructing a "memory palace" to finding your calm when you feel like you're losing your mind, the tips in these pages have got you covered, and will help you to maximize your study, minimize your anxiety and optimize your success.

Use this book as your study buddy – here to hold your hand when you need some guidance and to give it a high five when you're acing it. Not only will it walk you through various study tips, it also offers guidance on how to keep both your body and mind healthy. The following suggestions, advice and hacks will enhance all the hard study hours you put in, and they might just take you from *"I hope I don't fail my exams"* to *"I'm gonna nail my exams!"*

If you're walking down the right path and you're willing to keep walking, eventually you'll make progress.

Barack Obama

PART 1

Getting Going

Study Tips

Whether you call it revision, studying, cramming, reviewing, hitting the books or torture, sometimes the hardest part is actually starting. When the prospect of exam preparation looms, procrastination can be taken to a whole new level, as you decide you simply *must* make a mood board, alphabetize your bookshelf or sort out your sock drawer. This section will help you to bite the bullet and crack on. Tips on how to work smarter? Yep. New study techniques you may not have tried? Absolutely. Ideas to keep you motivated? You betcha. Ways to kick procrastination in the butt? Pow! Bring. It. On.

Plan your work and work your plan

When you're given your exam schedule, instead of freaking out, take a deep breath and start planning. A timetable will be your best bud in the following weeks and will help you to stay organized. It will ensure that you use your time effectively, keep your thoughts in order and keep the panic monster at bay.

So, where to begin? Figure out how many days you have until your exams, then write a list of the subjects you need to study for. Allocate certain days to certain exams and then split each one into time slots for different topics. For example, work on ecosystems between 9 a.m. and 10 a.m., followed by plate tectonics between 10.30 a.m. and 11.30 a.m. Be sure to assign more time to the topics you struggle with, and allow for breaks. If you don't stick to your plan religiously, don't beat yourself up. It's there to make you feel more in control, not stress you out.

Make to-do lists

Ticking things off your to-do list is SO satisfying. Writing a new list every day will work alongside your timetable to provide structure, decrease anxiety and serve as proof of what you have achieved. Make sure that your lists are detailed and broken into smaller tasks. So, instead of writing "study biology" and leaving it at that, perhaps set it out as such:

Study biology:

- Go over evolutionary theory.
- Do questions 1–10 in a practice paper.
- Look at genetics.
- Do a worksheet.

Prioritize the essential tasks on your list, so that if you don't manage to do everything, the most important elements will at least be completed. Having said this, be realistic about how much you can achieve in one day or you may feel disheartened if you don't tick everything off. (If you want to add something on your list that you've already done *just so* you can tick it off, do it!)

Be smart

Throughout the exam-prep process, you should set goals for yourself, but make sure that they are "SMART" (Specific, Measurable, Attainable, Relevant and Time-bound). Huh? Let's break it down:

- **Specific:** Break down your topic into sections and set out a clear outcome, e.g. "I want to learn all the physics equations in modules 1 and 2."
- **Measurable:** Use ways to find out if you've achieved your aim – perhaps test yourself with practice papers.
- **Attainable:** Make sure that your goal is achievable and not over-ambitious.
- **Relevant:** Don't waste time on topics that you know for sure won't come up in the exam. Focus on things that are likely to appear.
- **Time-bound:** Set yourself a timeframe – for example, "I want to have memorized all key dates of World War Two by Wednesday."

Just start

Fear of messing up your exams may leave you reluctant to start studying. You might be procrastinating to the max because the thought of actually sitting down and cracking on fills you with dread. *"What if I fail?"* Stop it! If you put the work in, it's unlikely that you'll fail. Overcome this negative voice in your head by getting started. The longer you leave it, the less time you'll have to prepare and the more likely it is that you won't reach your potential. Exam success is all about self-motivation – no one can do it for you.

Choose your workspace wisely

Make sure that the place where you study is comfortable yet functional. Not too comfortable, mind – you don't want to fall asleep (curling up in bed is a high-risk strategy). You'll need to work there in peace and quiet for fairly long stretches, so make sure the temperature of your chosen room adheres to the Goldilocks principle (not too hot, not too cold, but just right) and that it has good lighting (preferably daylight). Keep your work area tidy and free of clutter.

Working in a communal area – in the lounge with other housemates or in a café – is likely to be distracting. Your best bet is probably either a room you can close the door on, like your bedroom or a study, or the library. Varying these locations may also serve you well. A change of scene means that you can build up different memory cues – like sights, smells and sounds – that may jog your memory when you're taking the actual exam.

You know how you work best – if you like some background noise, play some instrumental music; if not, keep things quiet. Perhaps give your workspace a cute name, such as The Study Cubby, to make it sound more inviting.

Restrict social media

"I'll just have a quick look on Instagram... Wonder what Sam's latest post said... I forgot to retweet that thing..." NO! Do NOT allow yourself to be sucked into the social-media vacuum where, before you know it, you'll have lost an hour or seven of valuable time. Given that much of your studying may be done on an electronic device, it's best not to keep any social media tabs open in the background. Perhaps you could deactivate your accounts during the exam period – or ask a trusted friend to temporarily change your passwords, so you can't access them. If this sounds like social suicide, give yourself slots of time when you're "allowed" to look on social media, such as when you've finished working for the day. If this seems like an eternity to wait, maybe have a look during your lunch break – bear in mind, though, that you should allow time to give your eyes and your brain a decent break from screens.

Train your brain

There is some evidence to suggest that playing brain games, doing brainteasers and completing puzzles can help to keep your brain active and possibly even improve your memory. Things like crosswords, word-recall games and apps that focus on memory training are amazing ways to flex your mind – and they're fun too. Do them regularly and you may notice your concentration and problem-solving skills improving as well.

Adjust your routine

You probably know yourself well enough to recognize when you're most productive. Are you an early bird? A night owl? An afternoon sparrow? Arrange your study schedule around when you know your brain will be firing on all cylinders, then adjust the rest of your life around this. It's only for the short-term, so if you know you work better in the morning, make sure you have early nights. Similarly, if your brain kicks into action toward the end of the day, try to have a lie-in so you're well rested when you hit the books. Work on topics that you find challenging when you know you'll be most alert and least lethargic. If algebra right before bed works for you, so be it.

Select the right music

If you're the kind of student who can't concentrate with deafening silence, choose some music to act as a soundtrack to your studying. Research has shown that music actually stimulates both the left and right sides of your brain, which can enhance learning and boost memory. Listening to chilled music can also reduce stress by lowering blood pressure, decreasing heart rate and kicking anxiety to the curb. Classical music (think Mozart, Bach and Beethoven) might not be your thing, but studies have shown that it can help to categorize and organize information, which will be useful in your exam preparation. Listening to classical music can also help you catch some Zs if you're struggling with insomnia. For inspiration, search "study tunes playlist". Music without lyrics is preferable so that the words don't distract you and you're not tempted to sing along at the top of your lungs.

Mix things up

Don't plan to work on the same topic for hours on end. Your brain won't be able to take it! Instead, focus on one subject for an hour or so, then switch to something different. You'll be far more productive if you stagger your work this way. There's a good reason why schools, colleges and universities vary their timetables: people's attention spans can only take so much of the same thing for a certain amount of time (unless, of course, you're binge-watching your favourite TV show – that's different). If you try to learn about the same topic for too long, you'll probably find yourself reading your notes again and again, eyes glazing over, without absorbing a thing. It's better to work on a subject for one hour a day for five days than to work on it for five hours in one day. So, mix up your study topics to stop the snore-factor creeping in.

Complete past papers

It may be advice you've heard a million times before, but having access to exam papers that have been used in previous years is a real advantage. You might be able to spot a pattern in the topics that came up – and are likely to come up again. Studying past papers is particularly helpful in identifying the style and outline of exam questions. How are they worded? Do they require an in-depth answer? Are any of them multiple choice? How many marks are awarded for each question? Be aware, though, that there may have been changes to the curriculum since these papers were in circulation. If in doubt, talk to your teacher or tutor and ask for their advice. This being said, make sure you never get too cocky about what you *think* will be in the exam, because you never know what could come up.

Chew gum

As well as making your mouth minty-fresh, chewing gum could also help you crush your exams. Why? Studies have shown that chewing gum increases your attention span, raises alertness, improves concentration, enhances memory, reduces stress and makes learning easier. How? Breathing while you're chewing gum will allow more oxygen to reach your lungs than when you're breathing normally. The chewing motion also gets blood flowing to the brain, which improves its function. To maximize success, chew while studying, and also for a few minutes before an exam. Go for sugar-free gum to avoid a trip to your dentist after your exams are over, though. Chomp!

Put up sticky notes

Distribute sticky notes, with nuggets of knowledge written on them, all over your home. This way, you can learn while living your day-to-day life and make things "stick" in your memory. Make sure you put them where you'll see them regularly – on the bathroom mirror, on the fridge, by light switches, next to the toilet paper... (but make sure you have a sticky-note-free zone somewhere in your home – by your bed, at least; we all need to switch off sometimes). The more you read the notes, the more likely the information is to stay in your mind. Keep them short and sweet – no rambling explanations. When you're in the exam, you're likely to be able to recall seeing the note in its location (*"The Hamlet quote? I know this – it was on my wardrobe door!"*) more easily than if it was hidden among your other study notes.

Nothing will work unless you do.

Maya Angelou

Say things out loud

Do you ever read something over and over in your head only to realize you have zero clue what you've just tried to absorb? It's as if the information "goes in one eye and out the other". Multiple studies have proven that if you want what you're reading to sink in, you should try saying it out loud. So, whether you need to remember quotations for an English paper, equations for a mathematics exam or vocabulary for your oral language test, try speaking these things aloud to improve your recall. Just don't try this technique in the library – death stares from fellow students trying to concentrate may hinder your progress.

Construct a memory palace

A memory palace is a location in your mind where you can store images to recall as and when you need them, like in an exam. You'll create a "journey" through this location (often a building or town) and memorize different images at specific places that you'll visit in the same order each time. Create your own memory palace and you might just be crowned king or queen of the classroom. Here's how:

1. Choose a location that you know well, like your home or bedroom.
2. Plan out your route – for example: front door, coat hooks, kitchen, garden, etc.
3. Make a list of what you want to commit to memory – for instance, the first 20 elements of the periodic table.

4. Take each item on the list (in order) and place a mental image of it in a certain location inside your memory palace. Think of images that will help you remember the item. For example, you may use a star for "hydrogen" (the first element on the periodic table) because all stars contain hydrogen. If your first location is your front door, imagine a door handle shaped like a star. The second element is "helium" and your second location might be your coat hooks, so imagine a helium balloon tied to them. And so on.
5. Be creative, funny, silly – anything that will help you remember. The thing you're trying to memorize doesn't even need to have any relevance to your image. You might choose it simply because the word sounds similar – opting for a potato to remember "potassium", perhaps. Imagining your images interacting with your locations will also help them to stick in your mind. So, you might picture yourself milking a cow in your kitchen for "calcium" or shaking salt over your chips for "sodium".

Teach what you've learned

Becoming a teacher may help you with your exam preparation (although you don't have to replicate your history teacher's bad breath or channel your chemistry tutor's peppy personality). Not only will explaining things out loud make the information stick in your mind better, but you'll also be able to test your knowledge. Try to find someone who already has some concept of what you're teaching, so they can steer you in the right direction if you're getting anything wrong. They can also ask relevant questions to test your grasp of the subject even further. A fellow classmate would be the ideal person. They may even thank you for teaching them things they haven't yet got round to studying.

Put your phone out of reach

Can you resist everything except temptation? Having your phone right next to you when you're studying might prove too much of a lure for you. WhatsApp, YouTube, Instagram, TikTok, Snapchat, Pinterest, Facebook, Reddit, Amazon, Twitter – all just right there *at your fingertips*. How are you supposed to *not* sneak a peek? To remove the urge to look at your phone, physically remove the temptation by leaving it in another room. It's so simple but you'd be surprised how much more you can achieve without your phone staring at you, pleading, "Pick me uuuuuup." If you're in the library, bury your phone at the bottom of your bag so it's a hassle to get it out and check it.

Use diagrams and pictures

Many people work better with images than words and find them easier to recall in an exam. So, when studying, draw bar graphs, pie charts, tables or even silly pictures to help you remember the ideas, concepts, facts and figures you're learning. Mind maps – similar to spider diagrams – are also an excellent visual aid. Write down a subject heading or central idea in the middle of a page, then add branches around it to make connections. Do this at the start of your exam-prep process so you can study your way around the topics in a logical fashion, moving from one connection to the next.

Use colours in your notes too. Even if you're studying for your English exam where, obviously, words are paramount, you'd be surprised how effective visual cues can be. Just don't take too long making them works of art – they're not supposed to be an exercise in procrastination.

Think up mnemonics

A mnemonic is a learning technique that helps you to remember things by using abbreviations, rhymes or wordplay. They are a particularly useful way of remembering quotes, phrases and lists of information. A well-known example is a memory aid to recall the colours of the rainbow:

Richard Of York Gave Battle In Vain
(Red, Orange, Yellow, Green, Blue, Indigo, Violet).

Another (less cheery) example is a rhyme used to describe what happened to Henry VIII's wives:

Divorced, beheaded, died,
Divorced, beheaded, survived.

Have some fun when coming up with your own mnemonics – you're more likely to remember them if they're unique to you. And if they can make you smile, so much the better. Just try not to crack yourself up too much when recalling them during the exam!

Take regular breaks

All work and no play makes Jack a dull boy. It also makes Jack unlikely to pass his exams.* You may think that to achieve exam success you need to be chained to your desk working, working, working, 24/7, but this isn't actually the case. In fact, it is counterproductive. Without regular breaks, your brain will overload and steam will start shooting out of your ears, leaving you clueless and confused.**

Making time for breaks at various points throughout the day will allow your brain to absorb more information. Go for a walk, chat to your housemates, call your parents, have a snack, start sorting out your floordrobe... Whatever you decide to do, though, make sure your break isn't longer than your study session.

* Same scenario if your name isn't Jack.

** This *might* be an exaggeration.

Listen to a podcast

Whatever you're studying, chances are there's a podcast on that topic (or near enough – go have a look online). Even if it's not 100 per cent relevant to your exams, a podcast can help broaden your understanding and refresh your perspective, or at the very least give your eyes a rest from books and screens. Don't kid yourself that you can kick back all day with your headphones on, but don't rule out the benefits of a bit of audio. It's especially useful if you want to make the most of the time spent commuting or doing chores.

Keep your notes neat

No one is going to see your study notes except you, so they don't need to be pristine… but they do need to be legible and have some kind of order, so that when you look over them again (and again), you won't be left scratching your head and wondering, "*Huh? What did I mean by* that?" Start by looking back over the notes you took in classes and make sure you have a full set. Did you miss any lessons or lectures? If so, ask a classmate if you could borrow their notes (and return the favour if they are missing any). You may want to colour-code different sections of work that tie in with each other – for this you could use highlighter pens or coloured stickers. Use keywords as subheadings so you can navigate through your notes more easily. Bullet points are also a good idea, instead of long complicated sentences.

Practise managing your time

As well as learning to manage your time while studying (for example, not spending too long on one topic and neglecting another), you should also think ahead to the exam. Are you going to be able to effectively manage your time under pressure? When working on past exam papers, get into the habit of dividing up your time appropriately. This could mean allowing more time for the questions that have more marks allocated to them and perhaps answering them first, before moving onto the ones with fewer marks. Be sure to allow enough time for all the questions, though. Managing your time is an important skill, and the more you practise doing it before the exam, the better you'll be during it.

Use scents to your advantage

When you're studying, your eyes (for reading), hands (for writing) and bottom (for sitting on) are fully engaged. But there's another body part that could help you prepare for your exams and that you may be overlooking: your nose. That's right – certain smells are said to help improve your mood. They can also energize you, release stress and aid sleep, thus proving invaluable during your exam period. The following aromas may help in these specific areas:

- **To energize:** lemon, orange, rosemary.
- **To relax:** jasmine, clary sage, lavender, ylang-ylang.
- **To aid sleep:** lavender, vetiver, sandalwood.
- **To boost mood:** bergamot, mint, basil oil.

You could place a few drops of these essential oils into a diffuser, breathe them in and allow them to work their magic. Or go for the real deal and, say, eat an orange at your desk and leave the rind nearby so you can continue to smell it.

Make up a jingle

You know those annoying adverts that get stuck in your head, with a singsong phone number at the end? No matter how many years go by, you'll still know the number to call if you want a taxi/ home insurance/double-glazing. If you're trying to make key digits stick in your head, use this device of reciting them in a singsong, rhythmic fashion. You can even add some words (rhyming or otherwise) around the numbers to make it a full-on jingle. These ditties may be haunting you well into your sixties, but it'll be worth it if they help you remember what you need for your upcoming exams.

Put up a motivational message

Even if you're the most driven student around, chances are that your motivation may wane. We all need a little boost sometimes – a reminder of why we're doing what we're doing, and what our end goal is. This is where a motivational message can help. Choose a quote, a mantra or an inspiring song lyric, keep it on or near your workstation and read the words frequently. Some examples could be:

- Never do tomorrow what you can do today.
- Procrastination is the thief of time.
- Trust yourself: you know more than you think.
- You've got this.
- The harder you work for something, the greater you'll feel when you achieve it.
- Success doesn't just find you. You have to go out and get it.
- Do something today that your future self will thank you for.

I don't like to gamble, but if there is one thing I'm willing to bet on, it's myself.

Beyoncé

PART 2

Staying Well

Health Tips

It's no good being able to recite the entire internet if you make yourself so ill from studying and worrying that you can't actually take your exams. It's important to be kind to yourself during this time, which means eating well, sleeping well and doing everything you can to *be* well. A healthy body often equals a healthy mind, so looking after yourself means that your brain will be super-sharp and ready to absorb information. (Note: one of the tips in this section is to eat chocolate. Remember: healthful living doesn't *always* have to mean lettuce leaves and limbering up for a long run.)

Eat well

If you want your brain to be at its best, you need to make sure you're putting the right stuff into your body. Both your body and your brain need the right nutrients in order to perform at their peak. So, how can you munch your way to top marks?

- **Eat brain foods.** Certain foods give your brain a boost by improving concentration, increasing energy levels and heightening your ability to retain information. Try oily fish, such as salmon or mackerel, blueberries, broccoli, wholegrains, eggs and oranges.
- **Keep junk food to a minimum.** Foods like chips, cakes, sweets and biscuits may taste good in the moment but, since they contain little nutritional value, they won't do you – or your studying – any favours.

- **Eat colours.** A "beige diet" (think toast, chips, chicken nuggets, pizza, sandwiches and pasta) is one that won't serve your body well. Pep it up with some colour – cucumber, corn, carrots, tomatoes, peppers, avocado, grapes, watermelon, butternut squash, bananas... You get the idea. These foods are packed with valuable vitamins and minerals to help your body function at its best.
- **Darken up your diet.** Although bright colours will serve you well, adding dark-coloured fruits and vegetables – like blackberries, plums, leafy greens, prunes and pomegranates – is also a step in the right direction, as they contain antioxidants which play a part in boosting your immune system.
- **Keep sniffles at bay.** You don't want to be constantly blowing your nose while trying to study, so make sure you keep your body well fuelled with vitamins A, C, D and E – plus iron and zinc – which all help to fight off colds. Eat oranges, nuts, seeds, leafy green vegetables, and hearty soups containing beans and lentils.

- **Avoid processed foods.** Instead, go for foods with natural sources of vitamins and minerals. Fruits, vegetables, grains and legumes (like chickpeas and lentils) are a good bet.
- **Snack wisely.** Keep your energy levels up, and prevent your brain from powering down, with the following snacks: a handful of nuts, pumpkin seeds, peanut butter spread on crackers or an apple (keep the skin on, as that's where the brain-boosting stuff is). Actually, any fruit will help to up your energy levels, due to the naturally occurring sugars – far more effective, and healthy, than a sugar hit from a chocolate bar.
- **Go easy on sugar.** Although a quick sugar fix can be tempting if you're starting to feel sluggish, don't succumb. The little boost of energy that you'll get will be short-lived and the crash afterward will leave you lethargic.

- **Keep your blood sugar levels stable.** Eating fast-release carbs like cereal and bread will create a sharp spike followed by a drop in your blood sugar levels, which can lead to cravings for sugary foods. But slow-release carbs, such as seeds, nuts, wholegrains, peas and legumes, will help to keep your blood sugar levels more constant.
- **Have a decent breakfast.** You'll want to eat something that gives you enough energy for the day ahead. Porridge will do the job, as will peanut butter on brown toast.
- **Don't skip meals.** You might be absolutely rocking your revision: crushing chemistry, smashing sociology, going great guns on geography... but don't, whatever you do, forget to eat. If you do, your body and your brain won't be getting the fuel they need to function properly, so your concentration will wane. If you think it's likely you'll forget to eat, set yourself a timer.

Sleep well

No one is at their best when they're tired, so make sure that you prioritize sleep during your exam period (although this doesn't mean nodding off mid-study and dribbling on your textbooks). You may think that pulling all-nighters will help you to cram as much information into your brain as possible, but you'd actually be doing yourself a disservice, because your studying won't be as effective as it is when you're well rested. So, how can you best recharge your body and your brain?

- **Eat sleep-promoting foods.** Some foods (like oats, lettuce, almonds, potatoes and turkey) can increase your body's production of melatonin, the hormone that helps you sleep. Bananas can also help you snooze, due to the magnesium and potassium they contain – they're not called "nature's sleeping pill" for nothing!

- **Don't drink alcohol.** If booze is in your system, your sleep quality will be compromised. Sleep will be lighter and more restless, meaning that you'll be drowsy and less able to concentrate the next day.
- **Avoid caffeine, tobacco and energy drinks.** They all contain stimulants that make it harder to get to sleep.
- **Don't look at a screen right before bed.** The blue light it emits will play havoc with your ability to drop off.
- **Create a haven.** Make sure your bedroom is cosy (but not too hot – you don't want to wake up sweating), with as little light and noise as possible. If this sounds impractical – say you live above a restaurant, next to a bar or by a night-bus stop – you might want to invest in some earplugs and an eye mask. Thick curtains or blackout blinds would also be a wise investment.
- **Sprinkle lavender oil on your pillow.** A few drops may help you get to sleep.

Stay hydrated

Want exam success? Just add water! Drinking water is always wise, but when you're studying and need to focus, it's even more so. Water helps to transport oxygen and nutrients around the body, flush out waste and toxins, and help with digesting food. On top of this, staying hydrated improves attention span, livens up concentration levels and helps to prevent headaches. It's recommended we should drink around eight glasses of water a day, but sometimes this can be easier said than done. To keep yourself slurping throughout the day, fill a water bottle and mark 200 ml (6½ oz) intervals with a permanent marker. Include times of day next to each interval too, so that you know you should have drunk "this much" by 9 a.m., "this much" by 11 a.m. and "this much" by 1 p.m., etc. If you're not used to guzzling so much, expect extra toilet breaks.

Don't drink alcohol

Have you ever felt more alert and able to focus after a couple of beers? Didn't think so! How about the day after drinking – do you feel psyched and ready to learn? Nope, figured not! Alcohol has many negative effects on both your body and brain – memory loss, dehydration, vomiting and headaches, to name a few – so it's best to avoid it during this period if you want to do your best. Alcohol is also a depressant and can affect your mental health, making anxiety, depression and stress rear their ugly heads – and the last thing you need during exams is more stress. There'll be plenty of time to celebrate with a few brewskies or cocktails after your final exam (if you're old enough, of course). Wait until then or you might kick yourself.

Avoid certain drinks

The artificial flavourings and colourings in soft and fizzy drinks can make you hyperactive and unable to sit still, meaning that concentration levels will plummet. Energy drinks can have a similar effect and, if you have too many, leave you jittery and a bit “all over the place”. It’s a good idea to go easy on these drinks in general, as they’re not great for your health, but it’s particularly important to avoid them when you’re studying, so that you can keep your mind sharp. Try to limit your coffee drinking too. Although caffeine will give you a short burst of energy and focus, this will be fleeting and you’ll be left feeling sleepy afterward.

Health is a state of complete harmony of the body, mind and spirit.

B. K. S. Iyengar

Get your blood pumping

You know that exercise is good for your body (hello defined arms, toned legs and flat-ish stomach!) but how the heck can it help you to ace your exams? For starters, it can lower your stress levels. After a run, swim, cycle, gym sesh, yoga class – or whatever type of activity takes your fancy – your body releases endorphins ("happy hormones") which will leave you more relaxed, less anxious and able to sleep better. These factors will all help to enhance your studying. And if you can do some "green exercise" – physical activity done outside – even better. Being outdoors, getting some fresh air in your lungs and being mindful of the nature that surrounds you can massively help to improve your mood and reduce angst. It can also make you feel more balanced, content, peaceful and confident; so, if you can, venture to the park, the woods, the beach, a field...

You don't have to commit to a full-on sweaty-faced workout – in fact, little and often would be more effective. Even if you can't get anywhere particularly "nature-y", break up your work with a walk to the shops, a run up and down the stairs or by kicking a ball around in the garden... Anything that will give your brain a breather and your body a burst of activity.

Eat chocolate

While no one is suggesting taking a dip in Willy Wonka's chocolate river, a few squares of dark chocolate every day could help to sharpen your brain. Yes, really! Studies have shown that dark chocolate can help to reduce stress and anxiety, improve brain function, and boost your mood. Nibbling on the nice stuff could therefore leave you more relaxed and at peace. So, if you want your mind to be chock-full of exam-smashing information, make sure your mouth is (sometimes) chock-full of chocolate.

Drink tea

There are so many different types of tea in the world, and many of them have properties that can support a healthy lifestyle and help you to feel your best. Try any of the following and find a new brew to complement your study sessions:

- **Green tea** can offer an energy boost and is high in antioxidants.
- **Chamomile tea** has a calming effect and can help to chill you out.
- **Oolong tea** has been linked to lower cholesterol, reduced risk of heart disease and improved brain function.
- **Ginger tea** is said to have anti-inflammatory properties and can help to soothe your stomach. Some evidence suggests that it could also help to reduce blood pressure.
- **Turmeric tea** is high in antioxidants, and can help to fight infection and reduce inflammation.

Play tennis

As well as having a positive impact on your body (the all-over workout improves your balance, flexibility, speed, strength, stamina, coordination and mobility), tennis can also benefit your mind. Studies have shown that exercise requiring a lot of thinking improves memory and the ability to learn – and, because every rally is different, tennis is incredibly mentally stimulating. It also increases self-esteem and optimism. You'll need to use creativity, planning and tactical thinking on the court; these are all excellent skills and qualities that will help you through the exam period. Game... set... match!

Do yoga

Want to take a break from bending your brain? Why not try bending your body? There are loads of different yoga poses you could practise, but these ones may be particularly helpful when it comes to exam preparation, when you've spent all day sitting hunched over a desk. Look online for tutorials on how to do them safely.

- **Downward dog** sends fresh oxygen and blood to your spine, leaving you more relaxed and your muscles less tense.
- **Cobra pose** stretches the chest muscles, while strengthening your shoulders and arms. It's particularly helpful if you spend a lot of time sitting down, as this can make the muscles at the front of your body tight.
- **Child's pose** relieves neck, back and hip tension. It's one of the most calming, restorative poses there is.

Take fish-oil supplements

The World Health Organization (WHO) suggests that we eat one to two portions of fish every week. The health benefits of fish could fill this entire book (almost), but the one most relevant to your studying is this: including fish oil in your diet could improve memory, concentration and mood. You may choose to actually eat oily fish, such as mackerel, salmon, sardines or trout, or you may want to take fish oil supplements (far less smelly). Buy them from health food shops or in the supermarket.

Jump into action

Doing star jumps, or jumping jacks, before a study session will get your blood pumping and improve its supply to the brain. This means that your grey matter will be "switched on" and ready for action (namely: retaining as much information as possible). Before you begin studying, try doing star jumps, or jumping jacks, for one minute on, one minute off – for ten minutes. Then, throughout the day repeat this exercise a few times, especially if you feel yourself getting lethargic.

Take a bath

A dip in the tub doesn't have to just be about personal hygiene. Yes, you'll get clean, but having a bath may also help with your studying. Firstly, it serves as a break from the books, and will get you away from screens and devices (don't try to scroll and soak at the same time – it won't end well). Secondly, a bath will relax and refresh not only your muscles, but also your mind. Being submerged in water calms the nervous system, thus reducing stress and anxiety, plus it improves your mood and alleviates mental fatigue.

On top of this, warm water helps the flow of oxygen through the respiratory system, allowing us to breathe a little easier. Baths have also been shown to improve sleep quality, which, added to a greater sense of calm, will bring you one step closer to exam success. (Bubbles optional… but highly recommended.)

Anytime someone tells me that I can't do something, I want to do it more.

Taylor Swift

Take a proper break

As your exams get closer, you will probably be feeling a lot of pressure to study as hard as you can, as much as you can. More is better, right? Well, not necessarily. Even if you are taking short breaks, eating well, drinking plenty of water – and everything else advised in this book – there will be some days when the words just aren't going in and your concentration reserves are running low. If you're feeling like this and having a tough day, try taking a whole afternoon off. Yes, you did read that correctly. It may seem counterintuitive, but it could just be the best thing you can do for your mind and your studies. Go outside and take a walk, meet up with a friend and have a well-deserved catch-up or take some time to do something you really enjoy to blow off steam. Forget about exams for a little while, allow your mind to switch off from revising and cramming – and enjoy just being *you*.

This shouldn't be an excuse to avoid studying altogether. However, the key thing is balance. When you're working hard, it's especially important to take time to recharge the proverbial batteries. Listening to your mind and body, and learning to recognize when you need to take a longer break, is one of the most valuable life skills there is, as this helps you to stay happy and healthy, and performing at your best.

PART 3

Thinking Positively

Mindset Tips

Reading... Note-taking... To-do lists... Planning... Timetables... Learning... Remembering... Diagrams... Mnemonics... Testing yourself... Staying motivated... *ARGH!* Studying for exams can be a stressful, overwhelming time. But it shouldn't take over your life. You need to give yourself a break – both literally and figuratively. This section will offer ideas on how you can keep your thoughts positive, your anxiety down and your spirits up. You'll find that with happiness comes motivation, a will to succeed and a keen, healthy mind.

Reward yourself

Give yourself constant little pats on the back. Done a full day of studying? Time for a treat. Aced three practice papers? Gold star. Remained motivated even though the TV was calling you? You deserve a prize. Perhaps you'll treat yourself to a tasty dinner, watching your favourite film or a much-needed catch-up with friends. However you do it, rewarding yourself along the way will boost your morale and serve as motivation to continue working, not to mention give you a break from your desk.

Plan a final treat

You've highlighted, mind-mapped, spider-diagrammed, timetabled and memorized to within an inch of your life and, quite frankly, you're feeling a little tired of studying. Boost your morale by having something to look forward to after you've sat your final exam. Perhaps a trip away with friends, a theatre performance with your parents, a meal out with your girl/boyfriend, a spa day, tickets to watch a sports game... Or simply a Netflix marathon on your own with a pizza and tub of ice cream. Whatever it is, choose something that will spur you on and serve as an enticing reward for all the hard work you've put in. Hopefully, the promise of a treat will make the time go faster and, before you know it, "blah" will transform into "hurrah!"

Cuddle a pup

Or stroke a cat, feed a bunny, pet a guinea pig – it's up to you. Animals are a beautiful and healthy distraction from exam anxiety. Whenever you need a break from the books, spend time with your own pets or other people's (with their permission, obviously). It's been shown time and again that hanging out with animals lowers your stress levels and blood pressure (unless you're being chased by a lion, in which case the opposite is true). Plus, they're wonderfully free of human worries: they don't care about your grades – they just like you for you. You could also explain some of your work to your animal friend to see if you know it well enough – they'll love listening to your voice, even if you're lecturing them on inorganic chemistry.

Banish negative thoughts

"I'll never pass... This is too hard... I might as well just give up..." Does the voice inside your head tell you that you're not good enough? Well, you need to tell it, *"I AM good enough!"* It can be difficult to turn a negative thought into a positive one if that's not how you're feeling, but the first step is to realize that a thought is just a thought: it's not a fact. Negative thoughts that get repeated over and over – such as *"I'm not good enough"* – can hugely impact your confidence which, in turn, can affect your study. Once you recognize that a negative thought has no substance, you can challenge it and try to reframe how you see things (e.g. visualizing yourself passing the exam, rather than smudging your notes with your fearful tears). Your thoughts don't need to control how you feel or how you behave, so don't let them.

Breathe

Of course, you're still breathing. Phew! But perhaps by paying a bit more attention, you could maximize the benefits. There are many breathing techniques that reduce stress, promote calm and clear your whirring mind. Try the 4-7-8 technique to bring a little zen into your life. Ready?

1. Sit down.
2. Breathe in through your nose for a count of four.
3. Hold your breath for seven seconds.
4. Release your breath through your mouth with a whooshing sound for a count of eight.
5. Without taking a break, repeat this process three or four times in a row.

Use a mantra

Think up a mantra (a positive phrase) that you can repeat to yourself when you need a confidence boost. It can be as simple as "I can do this" or you can come up with something a little more specific. Repeat your mantra either in your head or out loud – some people choose to do it in front of a mirror. If you're struggling to think of one, perhaps take inspiration from these examples:

I am smart and I am prepared – I've got this!

I will ace my English exam.

No matter what, I will keep going.

I will turn my nerves into positive energy!

Don't compare yourself to others

Yes, Sarah's really good at English, Sana started studying months ago and Malik is constantly posting "study selfies" of himself. But none of this matters. Don't worry about what everyone else is doing; focus on yourself. Spending time and energy comparing yourself to others will only wear you out – you've got enough to be getting on with, without adding this to your list. And you know those people who seem super-confident and totally on top of everything? They're probably just as nervous as everyone else – perhaps even more so. Just because someone is bragging about how prepared they are doesn't mean they'll do any better than you. It's best to ignore everyone else's noise and concentrate on yourself.

Listen to upbeat music

If all that studying has left you feeling a bit "meh", pep yourself up with some cheerful tunes. Music is a powerful tool for lifting your spirits and decreasing anxiety, so create a mood-magnifying playlist that you can listen to whenever you need a pick-me-up. Go for songs that bring back happy memories, ones that make you smile and those that you just can't help but tap your foot along to. Add some motivational anthems in there too. Struggling for inspiration? How about these to get you started?

- "Don't Stop Believin'" by Journey
- "It's My Life" by Bon Jovi
- "We Are the Champions" by Queen
- "Don't Worry Be Happy" by Bobby McFerrin
- "All I Do Is Win" by DJ Khaled

Dancing around the room is also highly recommended.

Talk to people

With everything you've got going on at the moment, it's OK to feel overwhelmed. But it's not OK to keep your concerns to yourself. If you're feeling anxious about your exams, talk to your parents, your siblings, your friends or your teachers. They (whoever "they" are) say that a problem shared is a problem halved, so as soon as you've opened your mouth to talk about your worries, you'll feel lighter and better equipped to tackle them.

If you feel that your concerns go deeper than being nervous about your exams, you may want to seek professional help. Most schools, colleges and universities offer counselling support, so don't be afraid to use it. The counsellors are trained to help you when you don't know how to help yourself.

Don't beat yourself up

If you miss a study session for some reason, don't panic. Life happens and things crop up that might take priority over your work. Or perhaps you find that, no matter how hard you're trying to concentrate, you just *can't*. You're human, not a robot, and your mind doesn't always comply with what you want it to do. Instead of getting mad at yourself, think of a way to catch up on your study another time. For instance, if you had plans to see a movie and then have dinner with your friends at the weekend, why not skip the movie so you have a couple of extra hours to hit the books and make up for the time you lost?

Tidy up

Messy surroundings can heighten feelings of anxiety and claustrophobia, so make sure your workspace is jumble-free. You don't have to get too intense about it and keep everything on your desk pristine at all times, but aim to keep things neat – because working in a clear, tidy space will make your mind feel clearer and tidier too. Which is surely welcome when you're trying to fill it with enough information to pass your exams. If you feel things starting to pile up, use it as an opportunity to take a break from studying and have a quick tidy-up. However, don't use it as an excuse to procrastinate. If you think you might be guilty of this, set a timer for five to ten minutes, tidy until the alarm goes off and then get back to it.

Visualize yourself succeeding

Visualization is a technique used by many successful people – athletes, actors, entrepreneurs and, yes, those studying for exams. The idea is that if you can "see" yourself acing your exams, you actually will. So, close your eyes and picture yourself in the exam room. What are you wearing? Where are you sitting? Who is sitting near you? What can you hear? See? Smell? What expression is on your face? What is your body language? What pen are you holding? How do you feel? Try to create the scene in your mind with as much detail as possible. Then imagine yourself doing well in the exam, writing furiously, asking for extra paper, feeling happy with your answers and having enough time to check what you've written... If you can see it, you can do it.

Veg out

You simply can't study all day, every day. If you try, you'll experience burnout and your work will become about as effective as a chocolate teapot. So make sure to take guilt-free time to switch your mind off and do something that requires little or no brainpower every now and then. Binge-watch a TV show, listen to music, play computer games... By giving yourself time to completely relax and put your feet up, you're likely to be more productive when you get back to the grindstone.

The first step is you have to say that you can.

Will Smith

Avoid negative people

This is good advice for life in general, but it's particularly important when you're studying for exams and need to keep your head in the game. Negative people can zap you of your energy, motivation and confidence, which is not what you need at this time. So, block out negative people both in the real world and on social media. If someone is regularly posting things online that bring you down or make you feel upset, "unfollow" them for a while. If you get invited out to social gatherings that you know will be draining, say "no". Your real friends will understand and you can look forward to hanging out together when your exams are over.

Focus on your end goal

Ask yourself what you want to achieve by completing these exams. Sure, you know you want to *pass*... But have you thought beyond that? Do you need a certain grade to get into the university of your choice? To get onto a training course? To move onto the next stage of your career? Looking to the future and imagining yourself where you want to be can help motivate you to study to the best of your ability. It will give your learning a sense of purpose and will provide you with the determination needed to keep going – plus it will fill you with motivation and enthusiasm for what you're trying to ultimately achieve.

Remember: this won't last forever

If you're feeling frazzled and worried, and are tearing your hair out during your exam preparation, remind yourself that there is a light at the end of the tunnel. What is stressful now will be a memory in a few weeks, when you'll have new things to focus on. While you're "in it", things may feel all-consuming, like you're stuck in your own version of *Groundhog Day* – but hang in there. Think back to a different time in your life when you thought a tedious or unpleasant situation would last forever. It didn't, did it? Don't fret: you'll be out the other side before you know it.

Meet friends in real life

Although it's easier to keep in contact with your friends via social media (you can stay in your pyjamas, for a start), meeting them in the flesh is better for your well-being. You can't hug a screen but you can hug your three-dimensional pal – and a hug triggers the release of oxytocin, a hormone in your body that will make you feel warm and fuzzy. Laughter also has a mega effect – it releases endorphins ("happy hormones") to make your insides smile too. Laughing also increases the amount of oxygen going to your brain cells and triggers positive thinking. So, when you're deciding who to meet up with, choose friends who crack you up and those who don't shy away from public displays of affection!

Meditate

Meditation is a wonderful way to give your brain a break. It can slow down racing thoughts, calm your body and allow you to banish negativity. There are many different types of meditation, so hopefully you'll find one that works for you. Here are a few to consider.

Mindful meditation: This meditation encourages you to become aware of your thoughts, feelings and surroundings. The aim is to "be in the moment", and this is done by paying attention to "now". Find a quiet place, sit comfortably and close your eyes. Focus on your breathing, keeping each breath deep, slow and steady. Acknowledge how your body is reacting: the rise and fall of your chest or stomach, the sensation of air flowing in and out of your nostrils. If your attention wanders, bring it back to the physical sensations of your breathing.

Body scan meditation: All too often, our body and mind are in different places. This technique helps to sync the two. First, lie in a comfortable place. Then, imagining a photocopier light is gradually moving over your body, perform a mental scan from the tips of your toes to the top of your head, slowly focusing attention on the different sensations, aches and tingles you're feeling. By the end, you should feel more in tune with your body.

Reflection meditation: Ask yourself a question. It could be something like: "*What am I most grateful for?*" or "*What do I love?*" When answering, don't try to be rational, but emotional instead – focus on the feelings that emerge, rather than your thoughts, and sit with them, quietly, for a while.

Let it all out

During exam period, you might experience a mix of negative emotions: worry, frustration, stress, loneliness… and you might feel like you need a good old cry. So do it! Let your emotions flow, without feeling silly or guilty. As well as being an emotional release, crying can actually help you to recover your emotional balance, because tears cleanse your body of the chemicals that raise cortisol, the stress hormone. After a bawl, you're likely to feel calmer and less anxious.

If you're not a crier, you can express your feelings a different way. Creative outlets such as painting, drawing, writing or playing a musical instrument are often beneficial as ways to help you process your emotions. They allow you the headspace to work through how you're feeling, in a healthy, positive way.

Acknowledge that you can't learn everything

You might be getting yourself in a tizzy thinking that you'll never be able to learn absolutely *everything* you need to know. And you're right: you probably won't. The chances also are, you're not going to get 100 per cent in your exams. Once you get your head around the fact that you don't have to be perfect, you'll feel less pressure and won't be so tightly wound – and will probably perform better. In the exam, you will probably forget a few things or you may not explain your point as fluently as you would have, were you not time-constrained. But that's OK. All of these things are normal and will also happen to your peers. You don't have to get a perfect score to get good grades. Keep reminding yourself that you can only do what you can do.

Hang out with people who aren't doing exams

When you're taking a break from studying, it can be beneficial to spend time with friends who aren't in an "exam bubble". Perhaps they're at a different stage of their course or career, so have already done their exams, or their exams are yet to come. Either way, they will be able to distract you from your work and talk about things that aren't related to your studies. They'll also probably be less stressed, so more fun to be around. Being in the company of friends such as these will give your mind a proper break from studying and stressing.

Colour yourself calm

It used to be that colouring was a child's activity. Not anymore! As well as being an enjoyable exercise for teenagers and adults too, colouring in has also established itself as a tool to help calm a racing mind, as well as easing stress and anxiety. It relaxes the brain and is said to promote mindfulness by allowing us to focus on the present. There is an element of repetition and attention to detail in colouring, meaning that we are focusing on the task at hand rather than our wider worries. For some people, colouring can even allow the brain to reach a meditative state and drive out negative thoughts. There are many mindfulness colouring books available to buy, or you could print off some sheets from the internet. And don't worry if you go outside the lines.

Smile

Even if you're not feeling particularly smiley (going over trigonometry isn't exactly a laugh a minute), give it a go anyway. The simple act of turning the corners of your mouth up is a trigger for your brain to release endorphins, the body's feel-good hormones, resulting in a happier, calmer you. If you're looking for some smile-inspiration, scroll through old photos, listen to a happy song, look up some jokes, watch a sitcom, seek out some funny cat videos on YouTube... anything that will turn your frown upside down.

Don't catastrophize

Catastrophizing is when you imagine the worst-case scenario and your thoughts spiral into a negative pit. It's not just thinking, *"I'm going to fail my exams."* Catastrophizing takes worrying to a whole new level. It goes something like this: *"I'm going to fail my exams... Which means I won't get into university... Which means I won't get a degree... Which means I won't get a job... Which means I'll have no money... Which means I won't be able to pay rent... Which means I'll become homeless..."* And so on. Stop your fears in their tracks by challenging how logical they actually are. For instance, as soon as you've thought, *"I'm going to fail my exams,"* take a step back and switch your thinking to a more positive track. Try this instead: *"It's very unlikely that I'll fail my exams, but if I do, I can always retake them."*

Keep a gratitude journal

If you're stressed about your exams and your mood is low, try keeping a gratitude journal for a week and see whether it makes a difference to how you feel. At the end of each day, write down three things that you're grateful for. Maybe you got a great score on a practice paper or revised a new topic, or perhaps you received a hug from a friend, or the weather was beautiful. You can be as minimal or as expressive as you like, and it doesn't matter whether you write your thoughts down or just recite each item to your reflection in the mirror before you go to bed. Having a positive mindset is all down to your attitude, and getting into the habit of being grateful for the little things is a simple way to shift your perspective and see your life in a more optimistic light.

Focus on what's going well

Sometimes, studying can feel like shovelling snow while it's still snowing. You master a few pages of your textbook – but then there are so many more still to go. If you ever feel like you're not getting anywhere, remember this: you know more than you think you do. To keep your motivation up, write a quick list of things you've achieved at the end of each study session – like a reverse to-do list. When you're struggling, look back at this "I did" list to remind yourself that, actually, you're making progress and doing great.

I don't believe in luck.
I believe in preparation.

Bobby Knight

PART 4

Final Prep

& After the Exam

You're almost there. You're coming into the home stretch. It won't be long before you can cut loose and celebrate with your friends (or, you know, lie down in a dark room and breathe a sigh of relief) because your exams will be O-V-E-R. But, whatever you do, don't get complacent now and fall at the final hurdle. There are still things you can do to maximize your success. This section will serve as your countdown to Exam Day, and offer pointers on what you can do a week before the exam, the night before, on the day and after you've put down your pen. Good luck!

THE WEEK BEFORE

Make a checklist

Write down everything you're going to need on the day of the exam – you might include: a clear pencil case, pens, pencils, an eraser, a pencil sharpener, a calculator, batteries for your calculator, a maths set, a ruler, highlighters, a bottle of water, a travel pass, a university pass... Make sure that you have everything you need. A trip to the shops or a few clicks online may be required to guarantee you're fully prepared. If you're ordering online, make sure things will be delivered in time.

Plan your journey

Work out how you will get to your exam. If you are going to drive, plan your route and try to find out if there will be any roadworks or diversions to contend with. If so, what is your Plan B? If you are going to use public transport, check the timetable and pick a bus or train that arrives earlier than you need, in order to give yourself plenty of time. It could be a good idea to figure out a contingency plan if your train or bus gets cancelled or delayed – perhaps a family member or friend could be on standby for a lift as a "just in case it all goes wrong" measure. You might like to do a practice run so that you know how long your journey is likely to take from door to door.

Condense your notes

In this final week, give yourself less to go over by squishing your notes down onto flashcards and mind maps. You're more likely to remember smaller chunks of information on a flashcard than pages and pages of notes. Really focus in on the most important elements, grouping points together and summarizing key information as much as possible. By doing this, you're not only going through your notes again, but you're also making it easier to commit this information to memory. If you have reams of notes, you may have to be a little ruthless, but this exercise helps you to focus on the information you think is most likely to come up in your exam.

Don't forget your other exams

If you have an exam coming up in a week's time, it can be tempting to focus on just that one and push all those coming up later to the back of your mind. Don't do this! Make sure your later exams are still included in your study plan. As well as breaking things up and keeping your study varied and interesting, this means that you won't have a last-minute panic that you haven't done enough. Of course, it's OK to focus on the exam that's happening first, but make sure you don't drop the ball on your other ones down the line.

THE NIGHT BEFORE

Pack your bag

Make sure that you have packed everything you need for your exam. Check and double-check. Give your pens a quick scribble so you know they work (and make sure you have spares, just in case). Sharpen your pencils. If you're going to need a calculator, check that the batteries work. To give yourself peace of mind, you might as well change them for brand-new ones – it's better to be safe than sorry. Check what food and drink you're allowed to take into the exam; some sweets for a little pick-me-up might be a good idea, and a bottle of water to stay hydrated and keep your mind focused is a must.

Pick a power outfit

Never underestimate the power of small things. You might think that clothes don't matter, and you're not completely wrong – looking sharp in the exam isn't going to gain you extra marks. However, the psychological boost of feeling good from dressing well is definitely worth a shot. Remember, you also need to feel comfortable if you're going to be sitting down indoors for hours at a time, so think carefully. Consider what the temperature of the exam room is likely to be like. If it's hot outside, will the room be air-conditioned? On the other hand, if it's winter, will the heating be on? Wearing layers is probably your safest bet, so you can layer-up or layer-down accordingly. Sweating or shivering your way through an exam will only distract you from the task at hand, so try to avoid this with canny wardrobe choices.

Plan your perfect power outfit ahead of time and have it laid out ready the night before. That way you won't be rushing to find clean socks in a panic the morning of the exam. If you don't have much choice over what you wear, you can still prep your uniform as normal, but maybe wear your lucky T-shirt underneath or a favourite bracelet. Anything that puts you in a positive frame of mind – whether it's a bold colour or a special accessory – is going to help.

Set alarms

Even if you usually wake up naturally, don't leave it to chance on exam day. Set an alarm, then set another one. It's unlikely that your alarm will fail, but you never know. Your phone battery may die or you may have a power blackout in the night, so it's best to prepare for all possibilities. Knowing for sure that an alarm (or two) is going to wake you in time for your exam will probably allow for a better night's sleep too. It's one less thing to worry about.

Get a good night's sleep

On the night before your exam, you might be tempted to study for as long as you can so that you're extra prepared. However, this might do more harm than good. The later you stay up, the less you'll sleep, and the more stressed you're likely to become. One of the best ways you can prepare for the following day is getting a good night's sleep, so close the books and step away from your desk. Aim to have at least 30 minutes (if not a whole hour) of time to unwind before you go to bed – have a bath, read a book, do some yoga, chat to a friend or family member. Let yourself relax so you can drift off to sleep. You've worked really hard to get to this point; an extra hour of studying won't make much difference, but an extra hour of sleep definitely will.

Doing the best at
this moment puts you
in the best place for
the next moment.

Oprah Winfrey

ON THE DAY

Get up early

If you want to arrive at the exam cool, calm and collected, you don't want to be rushing around in the lead-up to it. Instead, you want to get ready in a leisurely fashion – without having to shovel toast into your mouth or run the risk of forgetting something in your haste. To achieve this laid-back start, get up early, and give yourself time to fully wake up and compose yourself. You might think that getting up earlier than usual will mean you'll be sleepy that day, but this is unlikely to be the case. You'll probably get a hit of adrenaline before the exam, which will keep you focused throughout. You can always have a nap afterward.

Have a shower

Although "wash" might seem like a strange tip, it's been said that people who shower in the morning are more alert, more productive, less stressed and happier – and it's good to be all of these things before an exam. A shower will revitalize you, and make you feel fresh, awake and ready to take on some questions. Even if you usually shower in the evening, change your routine and have one the morning of an exam. If you want to give yourself some extra get-up-and-go, choose a shower gel with your favourite scent – maybe tropical scents like mango or coconut to make you feel relaxed, or perhaps mint to make you feel extra fresh.

Eat and drink

Make sure you have a decent breakfast on the morning of your exam to set you up for the day. Then, depending on what time your exam is, ensure that you've eaten beforehand (whether it's a meal or a snack) – the last thing you need is to be distracted by your growling stomach. Make sure that you've drunk enough water too, so that you're not parched during the exam. Having said this, don't drink so much that you'll be needing multiple toilet breaks throughout. Finally, remember: as a safety measure, always treat your exam like a long car journey and visit the facilities beforehand, just in case.

Play a power anthem

Give yourself an extra boost of confidence by playing a song that pumps you up and makes you feel like you can take on the world. Sad, moody tunes begone (at least for today). You've probably got an anthem that springs to mind and you know works for you, but in case you need a few suggestions, how about one of these pumping tunes?

- "Roar" by Katy Perry
- "Don't Stop Me Now" by Queen
- "Confident" by Demi Lovato
- "Eye of the Tiger" by Survivor
- "Fight Song" by Rachel Platten
- "I Got You (I Feel Good)" by James Brown

Don't talk before the exam

Standing outside the exam room, waiting to be allowed in, can be agonizing. There will invariably be people discussing what lies ahead, some filled with nervous energy (*"Did you learn this? What about that?"*), some overly confident (*"I've got this in the bag... Why do you look so worried?"*) and some completely ill-prepared (*"I've done nothing! Tell me everything you know!"*). Try not to engage. You need to maintain a sort of tunnel vision and try to keep any nerves or stress to a minimum. Discussing a topic you're not totally confident on or listening to someone brag about how brilliant they are isn't going to help at this stage – and neither is giving someone a five-minute crash course. Close your mind to everyone else's chatter and distractions, and focus on the task at hand.

Focus on what you know

On the day of the exam, focusing on what you *do* know rather than what you *don't* is the only way to play things. It's too late to learn anything else. You've studied however much you've studied, and you need to have the confidence that what you've learned is enough. If you start dwelling on the fact that you don't know this or you're a bit fuzzy on that, your nerves will get the better of you. So, just take a deep breath, walk into the exam room and do your best. You've got this.

Put your phone on silent

Most establishments won't allow you to take your mobile phone into an exam, but if you can (or if it has to stay in your bag at the back of the room), make sure that you've turned it onto "silent" or "airplane mode" – or, even better, turn it off completely. You certainly don't want to be the person whose ringtone breaks the silence. Don't be tempted to keep your phone in your pocket instead of your bag, either, even if you don't intend to use it. Not only could this prove uncomfortable if the phone is digging into your leg, but, as most exams prohibit the use of phones, you could be accused of breaking the rules.

Own your nerves

Your palms are sweaty, your heart is beating a little faster and you have butterflies in your tummy. Feeling nervous before an exam can make you feel on edge. This is caused by adrenaline, which your body produces when it feels threatened. Although it's often uncomfortable, remember that adrenaline also heightens your concentration and performance – it makes you more alert, more eager, more "bring it on". Instead of being scared of this feeling and letting your nerves consume you, use this reaction to your advantage and knock your exam out of the park. It's showtime and you're ready to rock.

AFTER THE EXAM

Be modest

If you think that you absolutely smashed the exam, good on you! But try not to tell everyone how confident you are. Not only will you make others feel vulnerable, inadequate or apprehensive about their performance, but you also stand the chance of looking like a fool if you haven't actually done as well as you thought you did. So, for your own benefit and others', it's best to stay quiet and calm, and wait for your results. If you're feeling confident, it's likely that you *have* done well, which is fantastic! However, for now, it's safest to keep your self-assurance to yourself, if you can.

Don't dwell

Mulling over this question or that answer is a waste of time and energy. If you studied thoroughly and worked hard, your results will likely reflect this. As difficult as it may be, resist discussing the exam at length with your friends. Doing so will only make you doubt your answers, and they might also worry about their answers while chatting to you. A lose–lose situation. So, put this exam behind you and either go out to celebrate or go home and, after a well-deserved treat, start concentrating on your next one.

Ask for help if you need it

Sometimes, even when things are over, you can still find yourself in a spiral of "what ifs" and "I wish I'd done thats". This isn't good for your mental health, and if you can't seem to pull yourself out of your negative thinking then consider getting medical or counselling support to help you. These professionals will be able to offer advice on how you can adjust your mindset so that your exams won't feel like the be-all and end-all, and so that awaiting your results doesn't dominate your thoughts 24/7.

Put things in perspective

If you don't think the exam went well, try not to fret. If your results aren't good, you'll most likely be able to retake the exam down the line, so think about how you can improve your performance for next time. Remember that although it's disappointing not to have done as well as you'd hoped, it's not the end of the world. It's simply a bump in the road that you need to navigate. Many people have had less-than-perfect school careers and still gone on to be super-successful. Joss Stone, Richard Branson, Drew Barrymore and Bill Gates are just some examples of people who dealt with failed exams and low grades... but those certainly didn't stand in their way.

Conclusion

You did it! You got through your exams! Well done! You should be proud of yourself. Whatever the outcome, you did your best – and that's the most you can ever do.

Hopefully, you were able to use some of the tips in this book to make the most of your study time, to keep your mind and body healthy, to think positively, and to prepare for the exam day itself. And, whether you used one tip or a whole bunch of them, with luck this book will have helped you to navigate your exams with a little less stress.

Many of these tips are great to carry over into post-exam life too. Staying healthy, focused and positive – and making sure you're prepared for what lies ahead – are always good approaches to have, whatever life has in store for you next. Good luck!

Further Resources

The following websites might help with your studying. Most of them have apps you can download too.

www.goconqr.com
www.evernote.com
www.examcountdownapp.com
www.mystudylife.com
www.xmind.net
www.coggle.it
www.quizlet.com
www.todait.com

If you want to talk to someone about your exam stress, these organizations could help you:

www.samaritans.org
www.mind.org.uk
www.nami.org

You are braver than you believe, stronger than you seem, and smarter than you think.

A. A. Milne